20TH CENTURY MEDIA

1970s & 80s
THE GLOBAL JUKEBOX

20TH CENTURY MEDIA – 1970s & '80s
was produced by

David West ☺☺ Children's Books
7 Princeton Court
55 Felsham Road
London SW15 1AZ

Picture Research: Carrie Haines
Designer: Rob Shone
Editor: James Pickering

First published in Great Britain in 2002 by
Heinemann Library, Halley Court, Jordan Hill,
Oxford OX2 8EJ, a division of Reed Educational and
Professional Publishing Limited.

OXFORD MELBOURNE AUCKLAND
JOHANNESBURG BLANTYRE GABORONE
IBADAN PORTSMOUTH (NH) USA CHICAGO

06 05 04 03 02
10 9 8 7 6 5 4 3 2 1

ISBN 0 431 15258 6 (HB)
ISBN 0 431 15272 1 (PB)

British Library Cataloguing in Publication Data

Parker, Steve, 1952-
20th century media the 1970s & 80s: the global
jukebox
1. Video tape recorders - History - Juvenile literature
2. Sound - Equipment and supplies - History -
Juvenile literature
I. Title II. Twentieth-century media the 1970s & 80s
778.5'993'09047

Printed and bound in Italy

PHOTO CREDITS :
Abbreviations: t-top, m-middle, b-bottom, r-right,
l-left.

Cover m & bl, 8bl, 25ml - Corbis Stock Market.
Cover br - JVC. 3, 5bl, 6tr & b, 8tr, 9r & bl, 10tr,
14tr, 16tl, 17tl, 24b & 26b - Popperfoto/Reuters. 4tr,
11tl, 12 both, 15bl, 18m, 26tr & 27m - Popperfoto.
4br, 5br, 7br, 18b, 19t, 21tr, 22b, 28tl & tr, 29br - Vin
Mag Archive Ltd. 7tl, 10b, 23mr, 27tr, 28b - Topham
Picturepoint. 7m - Rex Features. 9t - Ed Young/Science
Photo Library. 11br - Sony. 13tl & tr - I.T.N. 13mr -
Mirror Syndication International. 13m - BFI Stills,
Posters and Designs. 13br, 22t, 23bl - The Kobal
Collection. 17mr, 23tl, 27b - The Culture Archive.
17bl - BSkyB. 19m (Paul Massey), 20tr (Richie
Aaron), 20bl (Tom Hanley), 21l (Ebet Roberts) -
Redferns. 19bl - Intel Corporation (U.K.) Ltd. 21br -
Frank Spooner Pictures. 24tr - Bridgeman Art Library.
25tr - Charley Murphy (computer graphics), Hames
Williams (photography) and Leonardo da Vinci
(painting), cover for Utne Reader, 34, July/August
1989.

*The dates in brackets after a person's name
give the years that he or she lived.*

*An explanation of difficult words can be
found in the glossary on page 30.*

20TH CENTURY MEDIA

1970s & 80s
THE GLOBAL JUKEBOX

Steve Parker

Heinemann
LIBRARY

CONTENTS

SHRINKING POWER
The early 1980s saw the first mass-produced personal computers for desktop use. By the end of the decade they were 20 times more powerful, five times smaller, and linked into the media telecommunications networks.

THE BLOCKBUSTERS
Blockbuster movies with global appeal became a tradition from the 1970s. Anyone who had swum in the sea – or even in the bathtub – could relate to the fear of being sliced in two by a huge shark.

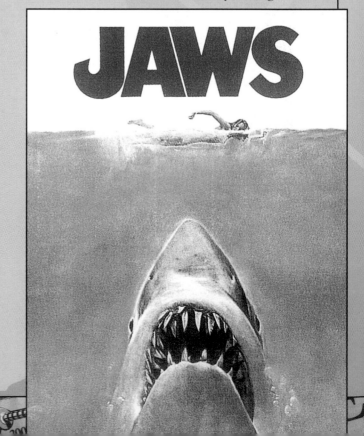

MORE AND MORE MEDIA

The mass media are how we find out what's happening in the world, and how we receive news, views, information and entertainment. In 1970, the main forms of news media were newspapers, radio and television. They also provided entertainment, interest, opinion and discussion, as did cinema, the print media of books and magazines, recorded music on vinyl disc and tape, photography and works of art. By 1990, this list had changed little. But choice and convenience had increased vastly. Extra radio and TV channels were on tap day and night, from space and through cables. People could record TV shows on videotape, to play later. A new format was the compact disc, at first for recorded sound. It soon became a storage device for a lump of electronics promising 'multi-media' at your fingertips – the computer.

WORDZ 'N' PIX
For economy, speed and fun, graphic designers loosened the distinctions between whole words, their abbreviations, initials and images.

FAMILY NUMBER ONE
The Simpsons helped to blur divisions between adult and adult – Doh! children's – TV. They began their world conquest in 1989.

FALL OF THE WALL
The opening of the Berlin Wall in East Germany was one of the media events of 1989. It signalled a new world order with the collapse of communist systems in Eastern Europe. Hopes rose for democracy, peace and freedom.

SPECIAL REPORT

Newsweek
THE INTERNATIONAL NEWSMAGAZINE

The Wall
1961-1989

5

EPIC SUFFERING

People who watched the scenes of appalling suffering on television, cried openly. Photos in magazines and newspapers, and radio reports direct from the area, brought a lump to the throat. Starvation, disease, hopeless life and gradual death were rife in Ethiopia, East Africa, during the terrible famine of the mid-1980s.

MOTHER AND CHILD
Just two lives in a relief camp for 5,000, but crowded with 22,000, on the Ethiopia-Sudan border.

MANY CAUSES

The causes of this huge humanitarian tragedy, which spread to neighbouring Sudan and Somalia, were many and complex. Farming in the dry, barren region had always been difficult. Years of attempted intensive agriculture had taken what little goodness there was from the soil, turning it to windblown dust. Then the sparse rains failed for several years. There was also political unrest. Warring groups fought for control and plundered the economy to buy guns, bullets and landmines, rather than food and medicines.

THE MULTITUDE
No shelter or sanitation, and precious little food, water or medical care – this aid centre in Korem Wollo province was one of dozens.

LIVE AID – 1.5 BILLION VIEWERS

One of the first media to campaign for famine relief was popular music. In late 1984, the UK's star-studded Band Aid recording *Do They Know It's Christmas?* raised both awareness of the Ethiopian plight and millions for relief efforts. USA for Africa did the same with *We Are The World*. Band Aid's mastermind, rock musician Bob Geldof, organized the 'Live Aid' concerts on July 13 1985. The trans-Atlantic fund-raising spectacular featured old and new from popular music, linked by the global media system of satellites, TV and radio networks.

Live Aid: London, UK and Philadelphia, USA (above).

THE WORLD WAKES UP

By 1984, the tragedy had reached epic proportions. Enormous camps were full of weak, ill and starving people, who had lost everything but a few ragged clothes. Journalists and TV crews arrived as usual to record their news stories. But even hardened reporters were so moved by the scale of the disaster, their voices shook with emotion as they described the awful situation.

THE PRESS GATHERS
On-the-spot journalists were often overcome by the horrifying sights, sounds and smells of the Ethiopian relief camps.

7

IN THE NEWS
For months in 1984–5 the situation in Ethiopia dominated headlines and reports in almost every medium.

THE RESPONSE

The world began to take notice. Especially powerful were images of skeletally thin yet swollen-bellied babies, innocently born into a nightmare of pain and deprivation. The media played a leading role. Campaigns were started to generate response from the rich nations, especially the industrialized West. Celebrities from music, movies, television, literature and other media spearheaded appeals for aid – both short-term food, medicines, tents and equipment, and long-term projects so that eventually people would be able to help themselves.

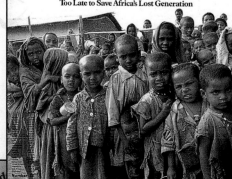

RAJIV'S INDIA
Can He Make It Work?

Newsweek
June 3, 1985   THE INTERNATIONAL NEWSMAGAZINE

We Are The Children
The New Wave of Sympathy and Aid May Come Too Late to Save Africa's Lost Generation

CABLE AND DISH

Coded radio signals travelling at the speed of light, broadcast from transmitters and tall towers, carry the pictures and sounds for television. These are picked up by the receiver aerials on our homes and other buildings. At least, that's how it was in 1970.

FROM SPACE

Satellites had been used from the 1960s to relay TV signals across continents and oceans. But the links were focused narrow beams between the very large, dish-shaped transmitters and receivers of the TV companies. The signals were then fed to the normal ground-based transmitter towers, for broadcast to the general public by the terrestrial system. But in the 1980s a new system arrived – DBS, Direct Broadcast by Satellite.

LIVE LINKS
Many technologies link on-the-spot teams with the general network. In 1981, this transmitter dish sent on TV pictures of the royal wedding of Prince Charles and Lady Diana, at St Paul's Cathedral in London.

DBS BEGINS

DBS is what most people now called 'satellite television'. Signals are sent up by the broadcaster to a satellite. This beams them down over a huge area, called the satellite's 'footprint'. The signals are powerful enough for small domestic dishes to detect. Anyone with suitable equipment can watch. NHK Japan began regular DBS transmissions in 1985. In Europe, the Astra satellite sent out Sky TV programmes from 1988.

EARTH STATIONS
Broadcasters send and receive radio signals for TV and radio via satellites, using huge dishes. A TV operator can receive specially coded signals from a satellite TV company, decode them and distribute them through its cable network.

EVOLUTION OF CABLE

Cable TV began in the USA in 1949, to provide good TV reception in remote regions such as mountains which were hard to reach by terrestrial signals. Gradually cable-based operators such as CNN (Cable News Network), MTV (Music Television) and ESPN (Sports Programming Network) joined with terrestrial and satellite systems and major networks, to share and re-transmit.

Bundling thin optical fibres into a cable.

CABLE GUY
The optical fibres could carry not only TV, but also radio, computer links, phone calls and on-demand movies or music.

UNDERGROUND

Yet another route for television signals is in the form of coded pulses of laser light, flashing along bundles of hair-thin glass rods called fibre-optic cables. These are usually laid underground and must reach every house individually. The USA led the cable revolution. By 1990, some 50 million homes were connected via more than 8,000 cable companies.

DIRTY DISHES
During the 1980s, concern grew that DBS dishes were ruining the view, especially on beautiful and historic buildings. New rules were introduced to govern their locations.

INTO SPACE
During the 1970s–80s, the buildings of big TV networks became festooned with large dishes pointing at satellites.

9

SO MANY CHANNELS

In the 1980s, technologies for delivering TV into the home leaped ahead. What would the extra hours of 'air-time' bring? Yet more news, current affairs, light entertainment and quiz shows, of course, but also ...

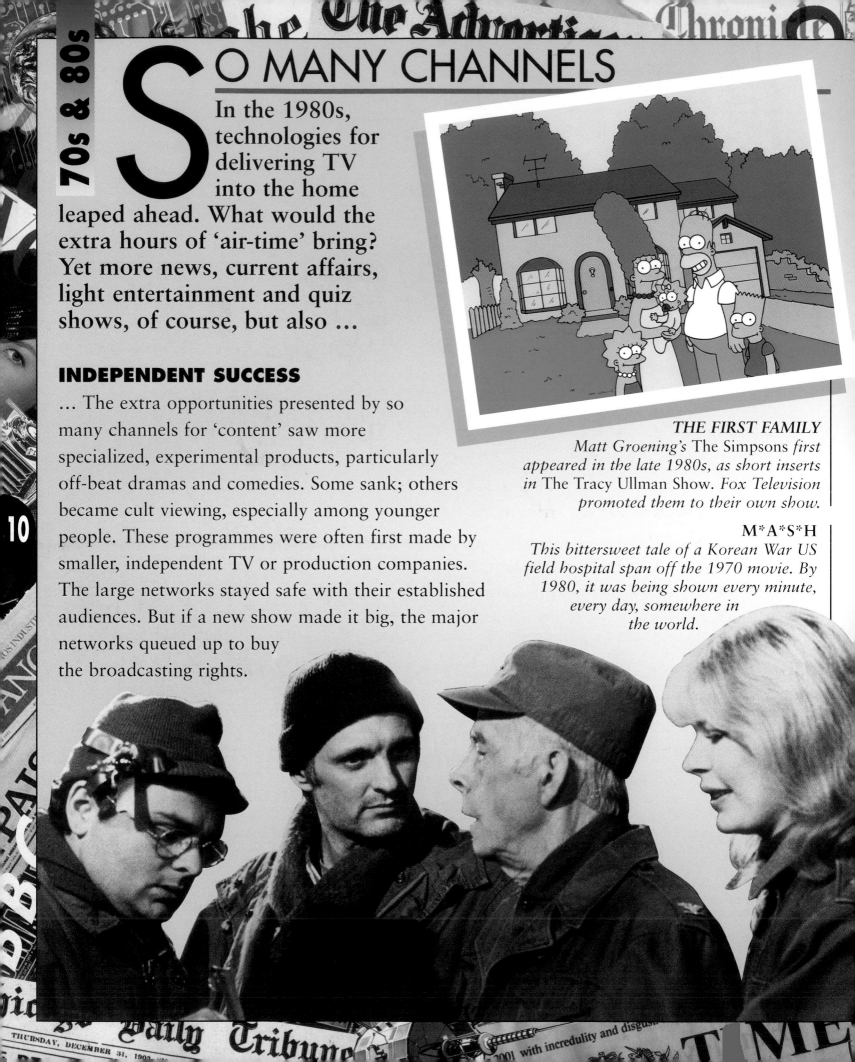

INDEPENDENT SUCCESS

... The extra opportunities presented by so many channels for 'content' saw more specialized, experimental products, particularly off-beat dramas and comedies. Some sank; others became cult viewing, especially among younger people. These programmes were often first made by smaller, independent TV or production companies. The large networks stayed safe with their established audiences. But if a new show made it big, the major networks queued up to buy the broadcasting rights.

THE FIRST FAMILY
Matt Groening's The Simpsons *first appeared in the late 1980s, as short inserts in* The Tracy Ullman Show. *Fox Television promoted them to their own show.*

M*A*S*H
This bittersweet tale of a Korean War US field hospital span off the 1970 movie. By 1980, it was being shown every minute, every day, somewhere in the world.

ZANY
Monty Python's
Flying Circus *was first shown
on the UK's BBC (1969–74). Based on
zany, anarchic humour, it poked fun at the medium of
TV with forgotten lines and false endings to shows.*

SPECIALIZED CHANNELS

Other results of extra TV time were specialized channels dedicated to one area of interest, such as the Discovery Channel, or a particular target audience, like the Children's Channel, or simple fun like the Cartoon Channel, or simply spending money with the Shopping Channel.

TIME-SHIFT

During the 1970s, video cassette recorders, VCRs, started to appear in homes. Magnetic videotape was already used by TV companies to record programmes for later transmission. Domestic versions allowed people to change their viewing habits by time-shifting – recording a programme while you were doing something else, to watch later. The TV and movie industries protested at first, but then cashed in by putting films on to video. The medium of television was becoming ever more flexible, convenient and all-encompassing.

FEATURE FILMS ON DISC
Several disc-based formats appeared from 1978, to show movies and similar long programmes on a TV set. They were based on CD technology (see page 14), and provided superior quality to domestic videotape. But ordinary TV-watchers did not flock to buy the systems, partly because they only played and did not record. (DVDs now fill this role.)

Movie laser-discs generated limited interest.

11

VIDEO
*The video
recorder-
player was
an exciting
new gadget
in 1975. It was
first advertised
mainly as a time-
shift device. But many
court battles followed, since TV
companies and movie-makers believed it would
be used for illegal copying.*

VIDEO WARS
*Sony's Betamax format gave superior quality to
JVC/Matsushita's VHS (Video Home System). But
support from the USA's
huge RCA
company, and
the economies
of mass
production, led
to a victory
for VHS.*

NSTANT NEWS

'We interrupt this programme to bring you a newsflash. A gunman has fired shots at the President of the United States, Ronald Reagan. Details are still coming in...'

GUN AND MAN
Reagan's would-be assassin was John Hinckley. He was quickly overpowered and the President soon recovered.

BODY GUARDED
Reagan was shot on 30 March 1981 near the Hilton Hotel, Washington, DC. Some bodyguards shielded him, risking their own lives, while others disarmed the attacker.

TELETEXT
Teletext systems became common in the 1970s. Signals for simple words and graphics are sent out with normal TV programmes, taking up a tiny part of the overall broadcast. Teletext displays them instead of the usual images and sounds, updated every minute or two. The viewer selects the content.

Current information by teletext.

IN SECONDS

Television crews and photographers at the scene recorded pictures of the event. Each TV channel is always monitoring the news of others. As soon as one channel 'broke' the story, others joined in within seconds. In minutes, pictures and accounts of the shooting had flashed by radio, cable and satellite links around the globe. The possible death of the world's most powerful man was so important, announcers broke into scheduled television and radio programmes.

'HERE IS THE NEWS'

News bulletins require intense effort by staff like producers, writers and videotape editors. As a bulletin starts, reports are still coming in, to be put together for its end.

AS IT HAPPENS

Television cameras soon became small enough for one person to carry. But a problem was feeding the pictures and sounds live into the telecoms network, rather than recording them inside the camera, to play back later. In the 1980s this was achieved by cable or short-distance transmitter link from camera to nearby vehicle, which in turn had a big dish for a direct satellite link.

Every second counts, both at the scene and in the studio. The stresses of working in the news media, and the good and bad effects this can have, were explored in several movies (right).

STILL GOING STRONG

Radio was far less costly to produce than TV. So radio could afford to compete by being more localized and specialized. Just a few hundred listeners might be enough to attract adverts and so pay the bills. By the mid-'80s, the USA had 9,000 radio stations – an increase of 1,500 on ten years earlier.

NEWS CONFERENCE

The world's media watch and listen at a press conference given by footballer George Best (seated left) and his Manchester United boss Matt Busby.

13

NETWORK

In this '76 movie a news presenter suffers a mental breakdown, ignores the script and threatens on-air suicide.

THE CHINA SYNDROME

This 1979 film follows the cover-up of a nuclear power plant accident and how the media help to find the truth.

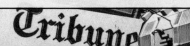 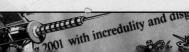

THE SHINY DISC

The compact disc, CD, is now a familiar format for storing music and sound recordings, also computer games and programs and files, photos and many other forms of information, or data. Back in 1982 it was very new, and some people doubted it would succeed.

A NEW FORMAT

During the 1970s many large electronics and media companies experimented with digital technology, where information is coded as on-off signals or bits, rather than as continuous up-and-down waves (analogue technology). Computers work digitally, and digital recordings could give much better quality, so digits were seen as the way forward. But in the medium of recorded music, there were already vinyl discs, and various forms of magnetic tape such as cassettes and reel-to-reel. Was there room for another format?

EARLY DOUBTS

Japan's Sony Corporation decided: 'yes'. By 1982, supported by Philips of the Netherlands, CBS and Polygram, they had produced their first CD players for a limited range of discs. The public were not so enthusiastic. True, sound quality was better, and you could conveniently skip to any part of the recording almost at once. But would music-lovers forsake their tape and vinyl players and huge record collections?

SHINY DISC
The micro-pits which carry on-off digital codes give the CD a rainbow-like, multi-coloured gleam. They are protected by a layer of ultra-clear plastic.

14

WHY THAT SIZE?

Sony's founder Akio Morita had long desired a convenient, durable, digital method of storing sound. Norio Ohga, who followed him as chairman of Sony, and was trained in music, advised that 75 minutes of recording would be long enough to encompass 19 out of 20 pieces of classical music. This amount of storage set the CD's size at 12 cms across.

'Mr Sony', Akio Morita.

ON THE MOVE

In late November 1984, Sony marketed a small, portable CD player, the D-50. They hoped it would become as popular as their radio-and-cassette-playing Walkman, and also revive the CD market. It did. The D-50 was quickly nicknamed the 'Discman'. Within another year the number of different musical recordings available on CD shot past 10,000, and the new format was here to stay.

THE FIRST CDs

CBS/Sony launched the first 50 CD titles, led by Billy Joel's *52nd Street* and including classical, pop and rock styles. One of the biggest early successes was Dire Straits' *Brothers in Arms* (1985). Its sales swept past 20 million and helped to establish the whole CD business.

15

IT'S THE PITS

Sounds on CD are stored as microscopic pits or depressions in the shiny aluminium-based layer. A laser beam pulse aimed at the surface is reflected by a flat area between pits, giving an 'on' or 1 of digital code. A pit scatters the beam and its reflection is not sensed, for 'off' or 0. The pits are in a spiral path, like a vinyl record's groove. Unlike vinyl, the CD plays from centre outwards. The whole spiral path of 3-billion-plus pits is 5 kms long.

Spinning CD

Flats between pits on CD surface reflect laser beam (red)

Prism lets laser beam hit CD

Lens

Laser

Laser beam is bounced off flats on surface of CD and is deflected by prism to encoder

Signals sent to amplifier

CDs ARE GO

CD players quickly moved from homes into cars (left) and as carry-anywhere personal stereos. An initial drawback was that the players could not record, as tape could. So many people ran the two systems side by side.

DT MM PC

The first desk-top personal computers (DT PCs) appeared in the mid 1970s. Designed partly for computer enthusiasts, some were even supplied in kit form! In 1981, business giant IBM introduced its PC and kick-started the march of computers into business, the media and daily life.

SMALLER BUT BIGGER
Toshiba's laptop of 1987 brought powerful computing for those on the move or away from the office.

A NOVEL IDEA

Computers are as helpful as the programs or applications and the information fed into them. Most people who had computer experience around 1980 gained this from work, using communal, sometimes room-sized machines. The idea of your own personal computer, available on your desk at any time, either at work or at home, to use as you choose, was a great novelty. Programs were very limited and, compared to modern versions, games and graphics seem almost stone-aged.

ADAPTABLE MACHINE

However computers scored well because they were adaptable or flexible. The same machine could be used for writing, accounts, design and communications (plus the occasional game). In the media, computers made a quick impact on the time-precious newspaper business. Using 'desk-top publishing' methods, one person could write the words, incorporate the pictures and design a page on screen in minutes – tasks that previously took several people several hours.

EXECUTIVE TOY?
In 1983, as early portables were launched, some people believed that computers would always be play-things of the rich.

REPORTER ON THE MOVE
Computer word-processors were ready-made for fast communication. Reports were already in electronic form, ready to be sent through the telecom network.

NEW PUBLICATIONS

The new ease of publishing encouraged many people to start up very low-budget newsletters and periodicals, such as 'fanzines' devoted to a particular star of music, movies or sports. Big media companies also started to send words and pictures between computers in their offices via the telecom network. This was the beginning of electronic mail, e-mail.

SCREENS GALORE
By about 1990, media offices, like those of many other businesses, were dominated, not by typewriters and designers' drawing boards, but by computer screens. This was a call centre for the Sky media group.

MOVING WITH THE TIMES
Computers allowed one person to do what many others used to do. Workers with old technology feared lost jobs. London saw violent clashes in 1986–87 as the traditional newspaper and printing region of Fleet Street declined in power. Papers such as the UK's first full-colour daily, Eddy Shah's *Today*, were produced using fewer people and more computers, at nearby Wapping.

Eddy Shah launched Today *in 1986.*

MM (MULTI-MEDIA)
In the late 1980s CDs were becoming the format for multi-media computer programs combining images, graphics, sound effects, music, animation and interaction by the user.

GOING MOBILE

In the early 1950s, the newly-invented transistor allowed electrical gadgets for media, such as radio, TV and recorded music players, to shrink greatly. The next quantum leap came with Intel's first large-scale integrated circuits, or 'chips', in the early 1970s.

SMALLER AGAIN

Integrated circuits are made on slices of a semiconductor substance such as silicon. All the electronic components – thousands of transistors, resistors and capacitors – are made ready-connected, or integrated, into one giant, complex circuit – but microscopic in size. With the advent of microchips, electronics entered another new age. Equipment became even smaller, lighter and less power-hungry, so that batteries could supply enough electricity. The way was open for portable, personal media gadgets.

AUDIO ANYWHERE
Personal stereos became common in the early '80s. They helped the popularity of radio, and also boosted the music industry, through sales of pre-recorded (and blank) cassette tapes.

FASHIONABLE
Despite worries that they could not record, the first 30,000 Walkmans sold out in two months. The gadget soon became a fashion item. Recordable versions date from 1982.

WALK, DON'T WALK

Transistor radios had been pocket-sized since the 1950s. The small, convenient cassette tape dated from the '60s. In 1979, the Sony Walkman combined the two with small earphones, for private on-the-go listening of recorded music or live radio broadcasts. A few years later the CD-version 'Discman' appeared (see page 15). These audio media now went anywhere that people did.

TALK, DON'T TALK

Shrinking electronics affected many aspects of daily life, from washing machines to computers. Telephones had changed little outwardly for decades. They were table-top units with wires to the wall. New chips allowed a radio transmitter-receiver, small yet powerful enough to fit into a hand-held phone, to link it to a local transmitter-receiver on a mast. Phones had lost their wires. The world and its media were going 'mobile'.

19

CLEVER CHIPS
Integrated circuit technology raced ahead during the '70s–'80s, packing millions of components on to a thin slice or 'microchip' of silicon a few millimetres square. Especially important was the CPU, the Central Processing Unit or 'main brain' of a computer. This doubled in speed and handling capacity, roughly every 18 months.

IC 'chip' in casing ————

Connectors to IC

Legs plug into main board ————

DAT
Some studios switched to DAT, magnetic digital audio tape. But domestic DAT lost out to CD. It could record, but not skip almost instantly to any part of the music.

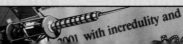

MUSIC REVOLUTION

New styles of music appear every few years, as each new batch of young people strive to be different from their predecessors. The '70s and '80s were no exception. As soon as a style became recognized and popular – another one was needed.

MARC BOLAN
The UK's 'Bopping Elf' led the early 1970s 'glam rock' band T. Rex.

OUTRAGE!
Pioneer punk-rockers the Sex Pistols burst on to the scene in 1976–77, in a flurry of swearing, spitting and loud, fast, very basic music. They outraged parents, the authorities, the establishment, and even music-lovers. Excellent!

GLAM, DISCO AND PUNK

In the early 1970s the glam (glamorous) rock of David Bowie, Marc Bolan and Kiss showed how sparkly costumes and spectacular stage shows could be as popular as the quality of the music. In 1977, the movie *Saturday Night Fever* shot John Travolta to stardom, and the Bee Gees' soundtrack helped to establish the soul-and-funk-based style of disco, with 'big hair' and colourful, flouncing costumes. Meanwhile, punk rock went back to basics with simple, aggressive, guitar-based songs for those fed up with glitter, fame and happiness.

ALL CHANGE

In the '80s it was all change again. Grandmaster Flash and Melle Mel's *The Message* (1982) brought rap and allied hip-hop, styles fermented in the USA, to a global audience. The synthesizer-based sounds of microchip technology and the baggy-trousered 'pirate' image signified the 'new romantic' style of Duran Duran, Spandau Ballet, Japan and Visage.

VIDEO

Mainstream rock was still in safe hands as '60s successes like the Rolling Stones, Pink Floyd and Fleetwood Mac continued their monstrous tours to an ageing audience, joined by the Eagles and Abba. The rise of television specializing in modern music, especially the MTV channel, led to the tradition of the 'promo (promotional) video'. This could be shown on a music show, instead of the artist turning up to perform live. Music videos quickly became an art medium in their own right, with lavish costumes and elaborate sets.

SUPERSTARS

Madonna was one of several singing-dancing-composing performers to establish themselves in the '80s and continue to superstar status. Her first global hit album was Like a Virgin *(1984).*

MUSIC EVERYWHERE

At the end of the 1980s, music, either recorded or on radio, was available almost everywhere. Kitchens, bedrooms, cars, pockets, belts, BMX bicycles, skateboards, school desks, windsurfers – all were homes to various kinds of players. More than 200 million CDs were being sold each year, far outstripping sales of vinyl discs.

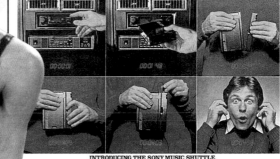

Combined in-car and portable player.

MUSIC VIDEOS

Music videos reached a peak with Michael Jackson's Thriller *(1983), from the 1982 album of the same name. It lasted for 14 minutes and, at $8 million, cost more to make than many full-length feature movies of the time.*

21

BLOCKBUSTERS

BIn the medium of movies, the monster hit of the 1970s which took more box-office money than any other during the decade, featured a toothy star with pointy fins and a very menacing soundtrack. Duur-DUR, duur-DUR …

THE AGE OF SPIELBERG

Director of *Jaws* (1975), Steven Spielberg went on to dominate the '70s and '80s with massively popular films such as *Close Encounters of the Third Kind* (1977), *Raiders of the Lost Ark* (1981) and *E.T.* (1982). Space was the major movie theme. Advancing special effects, computer animation, fanciful costumes and cute robots joined Luke Skywalker to fight evil Darth Vader in the *Star Wars* series (from 1977). Meanwhile, humans battled a stomach-bursting *Alien* (1979) and feature films were spun off TV's mega-successful *Star Trek* series (from 1979).

22

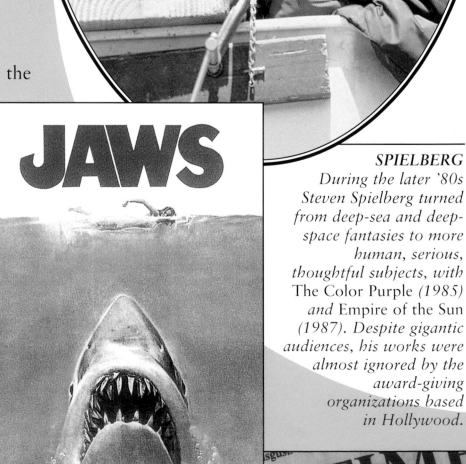

DEEP-SEA DANGER
Jaws *tapped into the basic, primitive human fear of deadly beasts from the dark depths. It included genuine suspense and jump-out-of-seat shocks, but little bad language and true violence compared to the exploitation 'horror flicks' of the time.*

SPIELBERG
During the later '80s Steven Spielberg turned from deep-sea and deep-space fantasies to more human, serious, thoughtful subjects, with The Color Purple *(1985) and* Empire of the Sun *(1987). Despite gigantic audiences, his works were almost ignored by the award-giving organizations based in Hollywood.*

An early multiplex in London, UK.

CINEMA FIGHTS BACK

Cinemas faced an uphill battle against TV, home-video movies and other growing domestic attractions such as computer games. Their response was to build multiplexes with five-plus screens, with a choice of features, more comfort, and opportunities to buy refreshments and movie merchandise. Like many Western nations, Britain's cinema visitors per year had peaked long ago, at 1,650 million in 1946. By 1984 this had crashed to 55 million. The following year the first multiplexes opened and audience numbers began to climb again.

REAL-LIFE THRILLERS

Major movie studios in the USA, relatively quiet in the '60s, hit back with big-budget blockbusters. *The Godfather* (1972) began a run of suspense thrillers mixing fond family life with the terror and murder of organized crime. Other movies dramatized real events, such as *All The President's Men* (1976). *The China Syndrome* (see page 13) dealt with a potential nuclear meltdown – as occurred the same year at the Three Mile Island power station in Pennsylvania, USA.

CAN'T SEE THE JOIN
Who Framed Roger Rabbit (1988) combined cartoon-style animation, using graphics and computers, with live action. Viewers were amazed at the seamless way Roger interacted with co-star, British actor Bob Hoskins.

23

SCANDAL
In 1974 US President Nixon resigned over break-ins and bugging of rival politicians at the Watergate offices. All The President's Men showed how media journalists helped to reveal the cover-up.

DOWN UNDER

Several other nations developed thriving movie industries, often with the help of government grants. Successful Australian films included *The Last Wave* (1977), *The Chant of Jimmie Blacksmith* (1978), *My Brilliant Career* and the first of the *Mad Max* series (both 1979). However Australian stars such as Mel Gibson were soon attracted to Hollywood.

THROUGH THE EYES

Computers spread during the '80s into the visual media such as graphic design, photography and printing. Computer programs could manipulate shapes and colours, with novel results. But traditional techniques still flourished.

SUPREME DRAUGHTSMAN

Born in Bradford, England, David Hockney (born 1937) rose to prominence in the '60s 'pop art' movement. During the '70s and '80s, he continued to produce beautiful works combining apparent simplicity, clean lines and bright colours, with exacting detail, elegant composition – and humour. His work reflected brash modern culture and advertising, and he also moved into set design for theatres and movies.

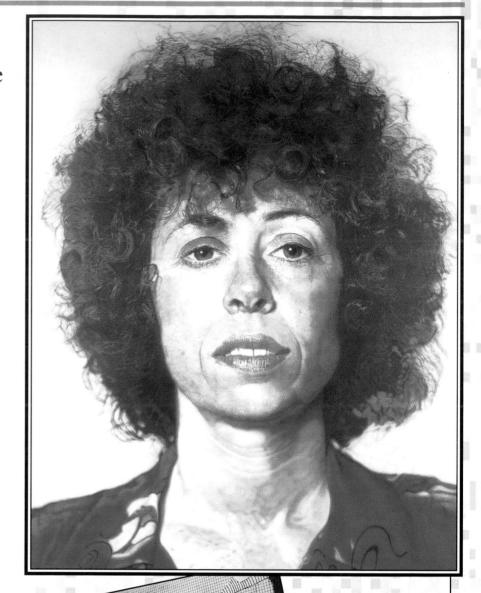

DAVID HOCKNEY
Leading British artist Hockney worked with photos, paints, silk-screens and other artistic media, as in sets for The Rake's Progress *(1985).*

CHUCK CLOSE
Most of Close's works are huge, detailed, realistic paintings of photos, usually faces. Linda (1976), is almost 3 metres tall. He also worked in pencil, and built up mosaic-like works from fingerprints or blobs of paper.

MULTI-MEDIA

Texan-born Robert Rauschenberg (born 1925) continued his '60s work with images from popular culture, included in his best-selling book *Rauschenberg Photographs* (1981). He experimentally combined techniques such as silk-screening, photography, synthesized sounds and theatre events into the medium of 'performance art'. Another US artist, Chuck Close (born 1940), developed the style of photorealism with huge, detailed paintings from colour photos.

GRAFFITI ART

Keith Haring (1958–90) painted the mural Crack Is Wack *(below, 1987) in New York City. Crack cocaine, a highly-addictive drug, became an increasing problem during the '80s. The message of Haring's wall painting was that drug-taking was a bad thing ('wack').*

ELECTRONIC ARTIST?

The computer was seen as a supremely flexible art tool – an electronic version of the paint brush. The way that it worked led to exciting new techniques, achieved on screen in a few seconds, making experiments much easier and faster. In the late '70s some people even suggested that a computer program could learn to paint, and so become a famous artist in its own right.

NOVEL TECHNIQUES

Computers greatly expanded the variety of visual effects available. For example, a conventional image like Leonardo da Vinci's Mona Lisa *could be pixellated – turned into block-like squares of uniform colours.*

MASTER OF GRAPHIC DESIGN

One of the world's great graphic designers, New York-born Milton Glaser (born 1929) has won every award in his field. His '70s book *Milton Glaser Graphic Design* remains a classic. Glaser's works encompass posters, magazines, newspapers, building interiors, company logos, record covers, typefaces and much more. In 1987, he designed the symbol and poster for the World Health Organization's international AIDS awareness campaign.

Glaser's use of the heart symbol for 'love' has become the most frequently imitated piece of graphic design in human history.

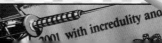

MEDIA EMPIRES

Bosses of media empires command enormous power. Wealth by itself brings great influence. Add to this the media's methods of mass communication, and a person can promote his or her views, opinions, businesses and ambitions.

NEW-AGE PRESS BARONS

The original media bosses were 'press barons' in charge of newspapers and other publications. As types of media grew, with radio, television, satellite and cable TV, movies and music, so did opportunities for a multimedia empire. For example, reports on a news channel can be 'selected' to portray its owners in a favourable light. Or one medium, like a newspaper, could carry plenty of favourable publicity for another medium, like a TV channel, in the same empire.

TED
Cincinnati-born Ted Turner (born 1938) built an Atlanta TV station into vast cable-satellite network WTBS, founded CNN, owned baseball and sports teams, and is a keen yachtsman and environmentalist.

BOB
Czech-born Robert Maxwell (1923–91) amassed a giant publishing group including Pergamon, Mirror newspapers and Macmillan. He died suspiciously leaving massive fraud and debt.

26

RUPERT IN THE '70s ...
Australian Rupert Murdoch (born 1931) started his country's first national daily newspaper, The Australian, *in 1964. He took over tabloids such as UK's* The Sun *and* The New York Post, *plus numerous magazines.*

NEW CHALLENGERS

TV in particular changed rapidly in the '80s. Stations, channels and shows were bought and sold. The 'big three' commercial US networks of ABC, CBS and NBC were challenged by newer groups such as Fox. By 1990, the Fox Group had seven TV stations, 120-plus associated companies, and links with newspapers and many other media.

TOO MUCH POWER?

In Britain, the commercial direct-broadcast satellite groups of Sky and BSB (British Satellite Broadcasting) challenged the duo of the BBC and ITV. Similar events were occurring in many other countries. One empire's radio, TV, publishing and other media joined forces to promote each other at the expense of competitors. Worries grew that too much power was being held by too few people. It could be used unfairly to obtain favours in politics and business, and influence voters in elections.

... AND '80s Murdoch went upmarket with the UK's The Times *and* Sunday Times, *purchased 20th Century Fox films and the USA's Fox TV, and negotiated for European Sky/BSB satellite TV. He became a US citizen in 1985.*

27

Silvio Berlusconi (born 1936).

SILVIO

In 1980, property developer Silvio Berlusconi began Italian TV's first national commercial network, Canale 5. More TV stations followed, along with Publitalia 80 advertising, the massive Panorama-Mondadori publishing group, department stores and great investment in Italian movies. In the late '80s, he took control of AC Milan soccer club, and aired plans to use his media to fulfil his political aim: becoming Italian prime minister. (He did so in 1994 and again in 2001.)

WRONGS AND RIGHTS

The media – especially TV, radio, the papers and other news-bringers – can be a tremendous force for good. Investigating reporters regularly root out crimes, cover-ups, corruption and injustice. These media can also be used as powerful allies by campaigners fighting for a cause.

SOUTH AFRICA'S ECONOMIC TREMORS

Newsweek
THE INTERNATIONAL NEWSMAGAZINE
September 9, 1985

WHITEWASH?
France's Greenpeace Report

NUCLEAR FREE PACIFIC

28

MEXICO'S EARTHQUAKE TRAGEDY
Making Cities Safer

Newsweek
September 30, 1985   THE INTERNATIONAL NEWSMAGAZINE

GREENPEACE
FIASCO

François Mitterrand
And Charles Hernu

Number 39

SCHEME BACKFIRES

Groups like environmental campaigners Greenpeace make skilful use of media to publicise causes. In 1985, their ship *Rainbow Warrior* was damaged and sunk by explosions in Auckland harbour, New Zealand. It was preparing for action against test nuclear detonations by France in the Pacific. Evidence soon came to light that the French government might be involved in the sinking. This led to fierce criticism of France, allegations of 'state-sponsored terrorism' and (despite losing a ship) great publicity for Greenpeace.

WARRIOR *SUNK!*
Greenpeace lost the Rainbow Warrior *but gained enormous sympathy and publicity, after claims that French secret agents sabotaged its anti-nuclear protest.*

DEADLY DARE
In 1987, another direct-action protest by Greenpeace was against burning and dumping toxic wastes at sea. Such daring stunts used news media to reach millions of people.

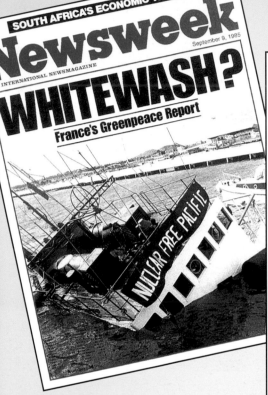

BAN THE BURN!
GREENPEACE

GROWING GREENS

Petroleum shortages and price rises during the previous decade had led to an 'energy crisis' in 1973, with giant queues at petrol pumps. This brought a new awareness of energy use and conservation as part of the blossoming 'green movement'. Most media played their part, by reporting the news, and also enabling commentators and experts to explain the problems and environmentally-friendly solutions.

MEDIA FREEDOM

In most democratic nations, the media are free to report facts and opinions, provided these do not infringe basic laws such as libel or obscenity. War is different. Giving out details of attack plans, or the location of planes and ships, could cost lives and help the enemy. In 1982, Argentina's forces invaded the British territories of the Falkland Islands, in the South Atlantic. Media, government and armed forces had to work closely together during the conflict that followed, to present news as fairly as possible – but not too openly.

The British media were carefully monitored by the authorities during the Falklands conflict.

BIG TROUBLES

But bad news continued. Acid rain, ozone thinning and possible early signs of global warming made big mid-'80s headlines. In 1986, a nuclear power station at Chernobyl, Ukraine, exploded in a mammoth ecological disaster. Another followed in 1989, as oil supertanker *Exxon Valdez* spilled a massive oil slick off Alaska. Despite many rights, would wrongs continue to dominate into the 1990s?

AIDS

In '84, Acquired Immune Deficiency Syndrome became a recognized condition, and its virus, HIV, was identified. Media campaigns alerted people to the risks.

BERLIN

In Germany, the fall of the Berlin Wall (see page 5) signified an end to the 'Cold War' superpower stand-off between the USSR and USA, with its nuclear threats. (From 1991, the communist-based USSR split into separate countries.)

29

AUGUST 12, 1985

TIME

AIDS

The Growing Threat What's Being Done

Virus, magnified 135,000 times, destroying T cell

SMILES AT HELSINKI
A Diplomatic Debut

GLOSSARY

BROADCAST MEDIA News and information sent out to many people – that is, broadcast – usually in the form of radio (electromagnetic) waves, as radio and TV programmes.

CABLE In telecommunications, a bundle of hair-thin fibre-optic strands that carry information in the form of coded pulses of laser light.

CD Compact disc, a format for storing information or data (pictures, words, sounds, computer programs and more) as microscopic pits on the shiny surface of a small or 'compact' disc.

COLD WAR The campaign during the 1950s–70s between the capitalist USA and Western nations, and the communist USSR and Eastern European nations. The two superpowers never fought directly in a 'hot war' but conducted their rivalry through the media and in third-party regions.

DBS Direct Broadcast by Satellite, where satellite signals are picked up directly by the receiver dishes of individual users, rather than by the dish of a TV network which then broadcasts the programmes by terrestrial systems.

DIGITAL A system that uses numbers or digits (usually 0 and 1) as separate or 'discontinuous' units, to code for information. The contrasting analogue system uses continuously varying up-and-down quantities or waves.

DVD Digital versatile disc, a format for storing information or data (pictures, words, sounds, animations, computer programs and more) as microscopic pits on the shiny surface of a small or 'compact' disc. DVDs hold 7–8 times more information than CDs.

PHOTOREALISM An art form where pictures are painted to look extremely realistic, almost like a photograph, as in the work of Chuck Close.

PRINT MEDIA News and information printed or otherwise put on to paper, as in books, magazines, periodicals, journals, newspapers and posters.

RADIO The general name for the sound-only medium which uses invisible electromagnetic waves sent out, or broadcast, from transmitter to receiver. 'A radio' is also the everyday name for a radio receiver or radio set.

TIMELINE

	HEADLINES	MEDIA EVENTS	MEDIA TECH	PERFORMANCE & ART
70	•*Students shot at Kent State University, Ohio*	•*Guitarist Jimi Hendrix, singer Janis Joplin die*	•*First domestic videotape machines: not much impact*	•*Rice and Lloyd Webber:* Jesus Christ Superstar
71	•*Greenpeace founded with great publicity*	•*USA: Musical benefit concert for Bangladesh*	•*First OMNIMAX cinema*	•*Kubrick:* Clockwork Orange *movie*
72	•*Ireland: British direct rule over Ulster*	•*Brando's long-awaited role as The Godfather*	•*First video games (played through a TV set)*	•*TV's long-running war 'sitcom' M*A*S*H begins*
73	•*Oil crisis, petroleum price rise, fuel shortage*	•*Led Zeppelin break all box-office records, Florida*	•*Newest hi-tech venue: Sydney Opera House*	•*Pink Floyd:* Dark Side of the Moon
74	•*USA: Watergate scandal, Nixon resigns*	•*California: 300,000 see British heavy metal show*	•*Berlusconi sets up his first cable TV channel*	•*Waterloo, first chart hit for Abba*
75	•*Horrors in Cambodia, Khmer Rouge run riot*	•*Bohemian Rhapsody by Queen with video promo*	•*Videotape 'VCRs' become common in homes*	•*Spielberg's Jaws breaks all box-office records*
76	•*South Africa: Soweto black township riots*	•*USA's Viking space probe sends pictures from Mars*	•*Fibre-optic cables come into use for telecoms*	•*Network movie portrays extreme media stresses*
77	•*Entertainer Elvis 'The King' Presley dies*	•*Sex Pistols and punk*	•*Apple II PC used for writing and page design*	•*Saturday Night Fever* •*Lucas's Star Wars*
78	•*Pope John Paul II elected*	•London: The Times *ceases for 11 months*	•*First laser-disc systems for home movies*	•*Grease movie musical*
79	•*UK: Thatcher is first woman prime minister*	•Alien *movie sparks rash of UFO abduction claims*	•*Sony Walkman personal stereo introduced*	•*First Star Trek movie* •*First Mad Max movie*
80	•*Ex-Beatle John Lennon shot dead in New York*	•*Italy: Berlusconi begins national commercial TV*	•*Ted Turner launches CNN 24-hour cable TV*	•*J. R. Ewing of Dallas shot to record viewing numbers*
81	•*UK: Prince Charles marries Diana Spencer*	•*Stylish new magazine The Face launched*	•*Gilliam's Time Bandits brings new special effects*	•*Spielberg's Raiders of the Lost Ark with H. Ford*
82	•*UK: Press under orders during Falklands conflict*	•*Michael Jackson's Thriller album 'most hyped ever'*	•*Audio CD (compact disc) launched*	•*Ridley Scott's future-movie Blade Runner*
83	•*Nobel Peace Prize for Poland's Lech Walesa*	•*USA: First episode of major glam-soap Dynasty*	•*CDs in most shops but take-up is slow*	•*Michael Jackson's Thriller video – many awards*
84	•*Ethiopian famine grabs global attention*	•*Maxwell is chairman of Mirror Group Newspapers*	•*CD 'Discman' boosts sluggish CD sales*	•*Madonna's first mega-hit album Like A Virgin*
85	•*Greenpeace's Rainbow Warrior sunk: sabotage?*	•*First systems for tele-shopping in USA*	•*Direct satellite TV to homes in Japan*	•*UK and USA: Live Aid concerts for famine relief*
86	•*USA: Space shuttle Challenger explodes*	•*UK: National newspapers Today, The Independent*	•*UK: Multiplex cinemas begin, audience returns*	•*Paul Hogan plays Crocodile Dundee*
87	•*UK envoy Terry Waite taken hostage, Beirut*	•*London: Violent clashes over new printing methods*	•*Domestic DAT, digital audio tape, launched*	•*Tom Wolfe: Bonfire of the Vanities novel*
88	•*Pan Am jet blown up, Lockerbie, Scotland*	•*Nelson Mandela's 70th birthday concert*	•*Direct satellite TV to homes in Europe*	•*Computers & live action:* Who Framed Roger Rabbit
89	•*Exxon Valdez oil spill devastates Alaskan seas*	•*London: Last newspapers produced at Fleet Street*	•*USA: Number of cable TV installations tops 50 m*	•*The Simpsons get their own show*

INDEX

32